It's A Pleasure
- It's Smiths -

A Pictorial History Of Smiths Imperial Coaches

It's A Pleasure
- *It's Smiths* -

A Pictorial History Of Smiths Imperial Coaches

Roger Smith

BREWIN BOOKS

Published by Brewin Books Ltd
Studley, Warwickshire B80 7LG
in 2002

www.brewinbooks.com

ISBN 1 85858 222 9

British Library Cataloguing in Publication Data
A Catalogue record for this book is available from the British Library.

Printed by Heron Press, Kings Norton, Birmingham.

Frontispiece: 1976 – LDA 500P a new Bedford YRT chassis with Duple "Dominant" 53 seat body.

Introduction

On December 31st 2001 Smiths Imperial Coaches Limited, one of Birmingham's longest established and most respected coach companies, closed its doors for the last time.

William Sampson Lloyd Smith (1894 – 1969) had been working for another charabanc operator called Pratt's and one day whilst starting his vehicle the starting handle kicked back and broke his arm. As he was unable to drive he was dismissed from his job, so in 1924 he decided to start his own business. Originally he had a business partner called Prentice, but this was short lived.

The first vehicle purchased was a Daimler with solid tyres and licensed to travel at 12 miles per hour! As with many early coach businesses the vehicle was used during the week as a lorry, a contract had been obtained to carry car springs from West Bromwich to the Morris factory in Oxford. At weekends the body was removed and replaced with a 28 seat charabanc body to carry passengers on pleasure trips to the nearby countryside.

Within a year the haulage side of the business was discontinued and Mr Smith concentrated on building up his charabanc business. Based in Imperial Road, Bordesley Green (His house at the time) the name "Imperial" was adopted for the company. One of the first bookings was by members of the Brighton Working Men's Club in Small Heath. With the low operating speed of the vehicle early trips were often to such places as Evesham.

The Daimler was one of the first charabancs in Birmingham to be fitted with pneumatic tyres and as a result was allowed to travel at the higher speed of 20 miles per hour. A second vehicle was added in 1929, a Maudslay 33 seater which was a much more luxurious vehicle having a "proper" roof and glazed windows.

In 1931 the company moved to larger premises on Stratford Road in Sparkbrook, the name of the company was changed to Smiths Imperial Coaches and at around this time Mr Smith was joined by his son William Gordon Dorien Smith (1914 – 1991) William was a talented musician, whose stage name was Billy Gordon. He played for the B.B.C. and won the Midland Amateur Accordion Championship and The Hohner Gloucester Trophy in 1936.

With the larger premises came more vehicles with Leyland chassis, having bodies by Buckingham and Burlingham's, added in the 1930's. A coach in those days cost around £1500 – in 2001 a new coach cost in excess of £180,000.

By the time the Second World War had started five vehicles were operated. The war years meant that pleasure trips were not operated and the company's vehicles were engaged to transport workers from Birmingham to a factory in Shirley. The War Department commandeered three coaches at £60 per week and when eventually returned in 1946 they still had gun mountings fitted to the roofs.

After the war the pleasure trips were started again and Weston-Super-Mare and London were amongst the first destinations. New coach bodies were difficult to obtain, owing to the demands placed on the body builders, so Smiths decided that they would have a go at building their own. Chassis were more readily available and in 1948 Smiths built their first body on a Maudslay chassis which was fitted with 33 seats. After this first successful attempt six other bodies were built between 1949 and 1950 on Maudslay, Leyland, Foden and a solitary AEC chassis

William Gordon Smith had spent the war years working at the Spitfire factory in Castle Bromwich and his experience gained there proved invaluable when designing the company's own bodies which looked as elegant as any of those being made by the major manufacturers of the time.

Separate premises on Golden Hillock Road in Small Heath were obtained in 1949 and a workforce of around eight were employed including carpenters, metal workers, upholsterers and a painter to produce these bodies under the name of "Gordons Coachcraft" – the designer's middle name. The skills used were not as scientific as today because the design was marked on the floor with the aid of a rope and piece of chalk, and the framework then constructed on the drawing. Another novel method for calculating where the top of the windscreen should be was to sit the driver in the cab and measure where the top of his head was. This worked fine for all but one of the bodies when the driver used was somewhat shorter than that of the others, this resulting in a shallower than normal windscreen! Plans to expand the body building part of the business were abandoned when vehicles from the mainstream suppliers became more readily available.

Many changes were made to the Stratford Road premises over the years, the original buildings consisted of stables and large covered sheds for the vehicles in the courtyard of a farmhouse known as "Priorsleigh", which is believed to have been built in the 1790's. In 1956 the outbuildings were demolished and a purpose built garage was erected alongside the house. The house served as the company headquarters and booking office until 1963 when it was demolished to make way again for a larger garage and workshops. The premises in Golden Hillock Road were disposed of in 1958 and additional land in Farm Road, adjacent to the existing premises, was acquired in 1962.

The 1950's and 1960's were 'boom years' for coach travel. Not many families owned their own car and coach travel provided a convenient and cost effective method of travel. Day trips to the coast and countryside were always popular and throughout the summer months coaches would convey people to their holiday destinations. Smiths ran services to all of the most popular resorts taking people away on their annual holiday. The coaches were also hired out for social groups, works outings and general pleasure trips.

Smiths became a limited company in 1957 and in 1962 Roger William Smith (1947 -), the son of William Gordon Smith, joined the company as a booking clerk and during the winter months worked in the garage helping to overhaul the coaches for the following season.

A major change in the company began in the early 1960's when inclusive coaching holidays were offered. These holidays were designed especially for the older traveller and were marketed as "Holidays for the Over 50's". A large clientele was established with many of these taking several holidays each year. An 'Over 50's Tourist Club' was introduced which offered members regular newsletters, special excursions and discounts on day trips.

At the end of each year, the company would hold an event to launch the forthcoming season's holiday brochure. This proved very popular and would include refreshments, entertainment and a free holiday raffle and for many years was held at Solihull Civic Hall. In later years the venue became The Tower Ballroom in Edgbaston where a Sunday Tea Dance formed the basis of the event.

The popularity of these Over 50's Holidays was such that regular travellers would start queuing at the company's offices from 6.00a.m. on the first day of booking for the new season's programme. Coaches would be parked on the forecourt for people to sit in and wait their turn to book. The holiday destinations mainly concentrated on U.K. resorts with Newquay, Falmouth, Eastbourne and The Isle of Wight amongst the most popular. The island of Jersey was also very popular and Smiths were one of the first coach operators to offer air travel to the island. In later years short breaks and tours covering most parts of Europe were also featured.

The holidays and day trips were extensively advertised at the company offices as well as through a network of agents throughout Birmingham. The boards along the front of the Stratford Road premises would advertise forthcoming day trips and holidays and a famous sight for over 50 years was the sign that proclaimed "Your coach is here Madam!" this was accompanied by a 'Flunkie' coachman who stood on the same spot until the end of the business. Over the years various other eye-catching signs were displayed such as a 1962 advertisement for private hire that read "Miles for sale 3/4d each".

Throughout the 1960's and 1970's the coach fleet was mainly based on Bedford chassis with bodywork by Duple or Plaxton. The late 1970's saw Ford chassis become the choice and by the 1980's this would be Leyland. Daf and Volvo chassis have also featured and bodywork from Van-Hool and Jonckheere of Belgium also joined the fleet.

Roger William Smith, after joining the firm in 1962, eventually took control of the company from his father in 1980 and became the third generation of the family to become Managing Director, in 1991 after the death of his father becoming Chairman. After working at the Stratford Road premises for nearly 40 years, Roger decided to take things a little easier and it was decided that after 77 years Smiths Imperial Coaches Limited would cease operating at the end of 2001.

Over the years Smiths immaculate ivory coaches will have taken thousands of Birmingham folk on many happy trips and holidays, covering millions of miles, and to destinations as far afield as Istanbul (Turkey) and Thessaloniki (Greece). Generations of families will have travelled with the firm and will no doubt have fond memories of their adventures.

The company will be missed by its loyal patrons and staff who can now only look back and say -

"It was a pleasure – it was Smiths".

Grateful thanks to Andrew Roberts for all his hard work in helping to compile this book from the many pictures in our collection.

Roger Smith – 2002.

www.smithscoaches.co.uk.

Fleet List 1924 - 2001

(listed in year acquired order)

Year new	Reg No.	Chassis	Bodywork	Seats
1924	OL…	Maudslay	Dennis	Ch28
1925	OM 6718	Daimler Y	Dennis	Ch32
1929	VP 7420	Maudslay ML3B	Buckingham	C32D
1931	OV 101	Maudslay ML3BC	Buckingham	C31D
1935	AOV 272	Leyland TS7	Burlingham	C32C
1936	BOP 503	" "	"	C32F
1937	CVP 513	" "	"	C32F
1929	VP 9531	Maudslay ML6A	Buckingham	C32D
1947	GOP 992	Bedford OB	Duple Vista	C27F
1947	GOV 959	" "	" "	C27F
1947	HOF 757	" "	" "	C29F
1947	HOA 542	Commer Commando	Plaxton	C30F
1948	HON 255	Bedford OB	Duple Vista	C29F
1948	HOA 528	Commer Commando	Plaxton	C30F
1948	HOP 626	Maudslay Marathon 3	Smith	C33F
1948	JOC 550	Bedford OB	Duple Vista	C29F
1948	JOF 332	" "	" "	C29F
1948	JOH 884	Commer Commando	Plaxton	C30F
1949	JOK 48	Leyland PS1/1	Smith	C33F
1949	JOL 998	Bedford OB	Duple Vista	C29F
1949	JOM 166	Leyland PS1/1	Smith	C33F
1949	JON 795	Maudslay Marathon 3	Smith	C33F
1949	KOB 100	AEC Regal III	Smith	C33F
1950	KOE 967	Bedford OB	Duple Vista	C29F
1950	KOF 860	Foden PVSC6	Smith	FC33F
1950	KON 100	" "	"	FC33F
1952	MOC 707	Foden PVRE6	Bellhouse Hartwell	C41C
1952	MOC 777	" "	" "	C41C
1954	OOC 100	Daimler CVD6	Burlingham Seagull	FC35F
1954	OOC 200	" "	" "	FC35F
1954	OOC 300	" "	" "	FC35F
1955	RHP 774	Daimler D650HS	Duple Elizabethan	C41C
1957	UOP 900	Bedford SBG	Duple Vega	C41F
1958	VOP 700	Bedford SB3	Duple Vega	C41F
1959	XOV 500	Bedford SB3	Duple Super Vega	C41F
1959	XOV 600	" "	" "	C41F
1960	800 BOC	Bedford SB1	Duple Super Vega	C41F
1960	900 BOC	" "	" "	C41F
1961	111 DOJ	" "	" "	C41F
1961	222 DOJ	" "	" "	C41F
1961	400 DOJ	" "	" "	C41F
1962	100 FON	Bedford SB5	Duple Super Vega	C41F
1962	200 FON	" "	" "	C41F
1962	300 FON	" "	" "	C41F
1963	333 JOH	Bedford SB5	Duple Bella Vega	C41F
1964	444 MOH	" "	" "	C41F
1965	COP 500C	Bedford VAL14	Plaxton Panorama	C52F
1965	COP 600C	" "	" "	C52F
1966	GOA 100D	" "	" "	C52F
1967	JOE 900E	Bedford VAM5	Duple Bella Venture	C45F
1967	JOF 800E	" "	" "	C45F

Year new	Reg No.	Chassis	Bodywork	Seats
1967	JOV 700E	Bedford VAM5	Duple Viceroy	C45F
1968	ROB 200G	Bedford VAM70	Duple Viceroy	C45F
1968	ROB 300G	" "	" "	C45F
1970	UOL 400H	Bedford VAL70	Plaxton Panorama Elite	C53F
1972	DOE 111K	Bedford VAL70	Plaxton Panorama Elite II	C53F
1974	ROX 800M	Bedford YRT	Plaxton Panorama Elite III	C53F
1974	ROX 900M	" "	" " "	C53F
1976	LDA 500P	Bedford YRT	Duple Dominant	C53F
1976	NWD 755P	Ford R1114	Van-Hool Mc.Ardle 300	C53F
1977	RDA 100R	Ford R1114	Plaxton Supreme	C53F
1978	VJW 600S	Ford R1114	Duple Dominant II	C53F
1978	VJW 700S	" "	" " "	C53F
1979	XVP 300T	AEC Reliance	Duple Dominant II	C53F
1980	FJW 400V	Leyland Leopard	Plaxton Supreme IV	C57F
1981	KOF 444W	Dodge 50	Reeve Burgess	C25F
1982	WBV 529Y	Leyland Tiger 245	Jonckheere Jubilee P50	C49FT
1984	B758 UHG	Leyland Royal Tiger	Van-Hool Alizee Super High	C49FT
1989	F100 COM	DAF SB2500	Duple 320SL	C57F
1984	A752 GBA	Leyland Tiger 245	Plaxton Paramount 3200	C53F
1990	BAZ 6528	Volvo B10M	Van-Hool Alizee	C53F

All vehicles acquired new – except the following: Previous owners: VP 9531 – Sugden, Birmingham, RHP 774 – Daimler demonstrator, WBV 529Y – Leyland demonstrator, B758 UHG – Leyland demonstrator, A752 GBA – Woodward, Glossop, BAZ 6528 – Shearings, Wigan

The following vehicles were re-registered: LDA 500P to UOC 427, RDA 100R to 154 YMA, VJW 700S to CIL 700 and VOV 96S, XVP 300T to YAU 400, FJW 400V to WOL 565, WBV 529Y to UDL 222, A752 GBA to YAU 400, B758 UHG to CIL 700, F100 COM to UOC 427

William Sampson Lloyd Smith at the wheel of a Maudslay charabanc owned by Pratt's of Birmingham – prior to starting his own business.

Worker's Union outing June 1925 to Cheltenham. William Sampson Lloyd Smith stands beside OM 6718 one of the first vehicles owned.

Smiths OM 6718 heads a line up of 6 vehicles on the same trip. Four of the hired-in vehicles are operated by White Rose.

Another early outing with OM 6718 which now has the name "Imperial" below the front windscreen. Note the maximum speed of 12 m.p.h.!

OM 6718 again, now fitted with pneumatic tyres – one of the first charabancs in Birmingham to have these.

Women's Pleasant Hour outing 1925 - OM 6718 is followed by two vehicles hired in from White Rose.

Women's Pleasant Hour outing 1925 - White Rose vehicle and driver.

Women's Pleasant Hour outing 1925 - Everyone all dressed up in their Sunday best!

Women's Pleasant Hour outing 1925 - OM 6718 One of the first vehicle operated by William Smith. It had a Daimler "Y" chassis with bodywork by Dennis seating 32.

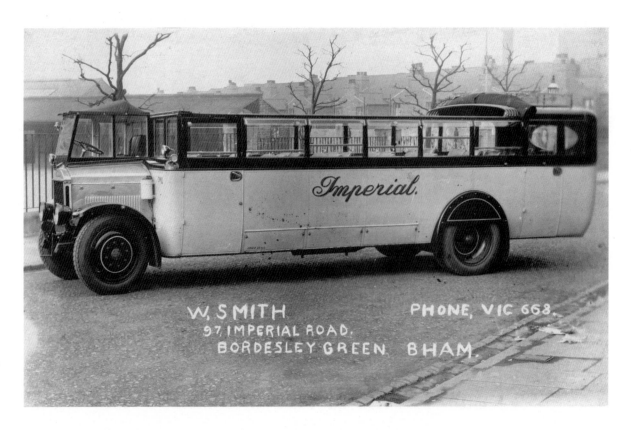

1929 – VP 7420 a Maudslay ML3B chassis with 32 seat body by Buckingham complete with full-length sun roof!

A later view of VP 7420 with a new roof and curtains fitted.

VP 7420 on the Stratford Road outside the then new garage and booking office. The high wall that originally surrounded the property can just be seen.

A view of 180-182 Stratford Road in 1937 when under-ground fuel tanks were being installed. The boards on the front advertise forthcoming trips including Ascot for 12/6d and a trip to France for 25 shillings.

W.S.L. Smith and friends.

A view of the completed forecourt with new petrol pumps. W.S.L. Smith, in the cap, looks on whilst his son, W.G. Smith is in the MG just behind.

1931 – OV 101 a Maudslay ML3BC chassis with 31 seat bodywork by Buckingham. It is believed that this vehicle later received a new body by Burlingham.

"Day trippers" late 1930's. Not much is known about these pictures as they were only discovered just in time to be included in this book. One of the vehicles is AOV 272.

"The Coaches with the Musical Hooters"

SMITH'S IMPERIAL COACHES
180, STRATFORD ROAD, SPARKBROOK, BIRMINGHAM
PHONE : VIC. 0668

1935 – AOV 272 a Leyland TS7 chassis with Buckingham 32 seat body. A number of Smiths vehicles around this time had "musical hooters". These were fitted after W.S.L. Smith heard similar horns on buses whilst on holiday in Switzerland.

Another view of AOV 272 this time all decorated for the Coronation of George VI in 1937.

Day trippers pose for the camera, late 1930's / early 1940's. Fred Brough, a long serving driver, was driving one of the Burlingham bodied Leyland TS7's.

Ernie Swain (in shorts) was the nephew of W.S.L. Smith - for a time he was General Manager of the company until his premature death in the late 1940's.

Smiths driver's annual outing – 1948.

W.S.L. Smith driving a Jackson, one of a small collection of vintage cars once owned.

1948 – HOP 626 the first coach body designed and built by the company. It seated 33 and was built upon a Maudslay Marathon 3 chassis.

Interior view of HOP 626.

1949 – JOK 48 Smiths second coach body, built on a Leyland PS1/1 chassis.

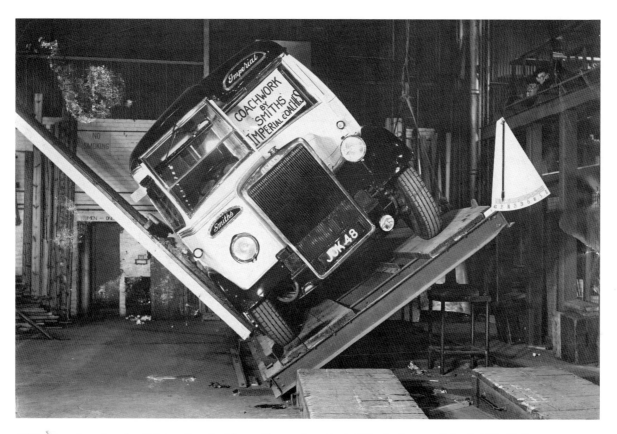

JOK 48 undergoing the "tilt test" at the Metro Cammel works in Birmingham on March 15th 1949.

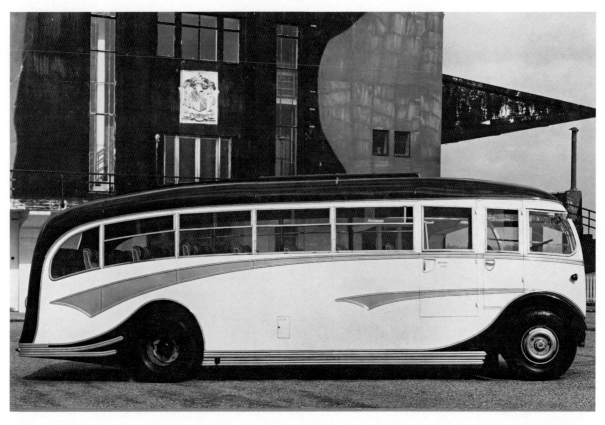

Another view of JOK 48, taken at Elmdon Airport which still has its war-time camouflage. Note the curved window line compared with the first body made.

A view of the interior of JOK 48 – all hand-made by Smiths bodybuilding team.

A rear view of JOK 48 showing the single piece, hand-beaten, rear panels.

W.S.L. Smith driving JOK 616, an 1898 Star. This car was donated to the Birmingham Science Museum and can now be seen at the new "Millennium Point".

The drivers and some of the fleet lined up for the camera at Hall Green Stadium in 1949.

W.S.L. Smith and W.G. Smith with some of the drivers at Hall Green Stadium 1949.

1949 – JOM 166 the third coach body built by Smiths, another 33 seater on a Leyland PS1/1 chassis.

Interior of JOM 166 – the height of luxury created by Smiths own employees.

Another view of JOM 166, brand-new and looking just as stylish as any of the bodies built by the large commercial body building concerns.

1949 – JON 795 a Maudslay Marathon 3 chassis with the fourth body built by Smiths.

A rear view of JON 795 at a typical excursion destination.

SUGGESTED TOURS
FOR YOUR
PRIVATE PARTY

WITH

SMITHS
IMPERIAL COACHES

180/182, STRATFORD ROAD
S P A R K B R O O K   1 1
'Phone: VIC. 0668

A brochure produced in 1949 with suggested itineraries and destinations for private party organisers.

DAY TOURS

13 CRANHAM WOODS. Bromsgrove, Droitwich, Worcester, Kempsey, Tewkesbury, Cheltenham Spa, Cranham Woods, Birdlip, Gloucester, Tewkesbury, Sedgeberrow, Evesham, Alcester.

14 HEREFORD. Bromsgrove, Droitwich, Worcester, Bromyard, Stoke Lacey, Hereford, Ledbury, Eastnor Castle, Tewkesbury, Evesham, Alcester, Studley,

15 MATLOCK AND DOVEDALE. Lichfield, Burton-on-Trent, Derby, Belper, Ambergate, Matlock, Matlock Bath, Ashbourne, Dovedale, Uttoxeter, Abbots Bromley, Lichfield.

16 SYMONDS YAT. Bromsgrove, Droitwich, Worcester, Malvern, Ledbury, Ross-on-Wye, Symonds Yat, Gloucester, Tewkesbury, Evesham, Alcester.

Page Five

Example of day tour destinations within 1949 brochure for private parties.

**33-SEATER LUXURY COACH BODY BY GORDONS COACHCRAFT LIMITED
199, GOLDEN HILLOCK ROAD, BIRMINGHAM, 11. VIC. 2959**

1949 – KOB 100 The fifth coach built by Smiths under the name of "Gordon's Coachcraft"
– Gordon being taken from William Gordon Smith who designed all of the bodies that were made.

**33-SEATER LUXURY COACH BODY BY GORDONS COACHCRAFT LIMITED
199, GOLDEN HILLOCK ROAD, BIRMINGHAM, 11. VIC. 2959**

A side view of KOB 100 which shows the curved lines of the body. A template was created on the workshop floor by swinging a rope with a piece of chalk attached to the end.

33-SEATER LUXURY COACH BODY BY GORDONS COACHCRAFT LIMITED
199, GOLDEN HILLOCK ROAD, BIRMINGHAM, 11. VIC. 2959

KOB 100 was the only body built by Smiths on an AEC chassis. It was a Regal III and would be one of only two AEC's ever operated.

Passengers pose for the camera in Llangollen in 1949. Drivers, George Meredith and Sid Hopkins, can be seen in their white driving coats.

Besides building their own coaches Smiths also took delivery of several other coaches during the late 1940's. Seven Bedford OB chassis with Duple "Vista" bodies were purchased between 1948 and 1950.

KOE 967 dates from 1950 with 29 seat body and was the last of the type purchased.

JOF 332 is a 1948 delivery with 29 seat body which did not have the normal side flare below the window line. This was apparently owing to a shortage of materials which led to this feature being omitted by the bodybuilder for some vehicles built in 1948 and 1949.

1950 – KOF 860 a Foden PVSC6 chassis.

KOF 860 was Smiths sixth body and was the first to be built with a "full fronted" design.

1950 – KON 100 the seventh and final body built. This was also a Foden PVSC6 chassis with a similar body style to KOF 860 but with more adventurous frontal styling.

A rear view of KON 100 - The rear panels are a real work of art!

An early 1950's view of the garage and booking office on Stratford Road, Sparkbrook.

Father Christmas arrives at one of Smiths agents - "College's" in Baldwins Lane, Hall Green. He is travelling in a Jackson being driven by Peter Turner a director of Smiths and son-in law of W.S.L. Smith.

SMITHS' IMPERIAL COACHES

180 STRATFORD ROAD, BIRMINGHAM II.

Phone VIC. 0668

Programme of Tours for August and September

| EVERY MONDAY, TUESDAY, WEDNESDAY and THURSDAY starting at 2.30 p.m. |
| 120 Miles Mystery Tour arriving home at 9.30 p.m. |

Mon	Aug	19	Day Trip to Skegness	Start	7.30 a.m.
Tue	"	20	" " " Weston-Super-Mare	"	7.30 a.m.
Thur	"	22	" " " Southport	"	7.30 a.m.

Friday, Saturday & Sunday—reserved

Mon	Aug	26	Day Trip to Colwyn Bay	"	7.30 a.m.
Tue	"	27	Grand Day Tour to Weston-Super-Mare and Cheddar Gorge and Caves	"	7.30 a.m.
Wed	"	28	Day Trip to Clevedon	"	7.30 a.m.
Thur	"	29	" " " Rhyl	"	7.30 a.m.

Friday, Saturday, Sunday & Monday reserved

Tue	Sept	3	Grand Full Day Mystery Tour	"	8.00 a.m.
Wed	"	4	Grand Day Tour to Windsor and the Thames Valley	"	8.00 a.m.
Thur	"	5	Day Trip to Aberystwyth	"	7.30 a.m.

Friday, Saturday and Sunday—reserved

Mon	Sept	9	Day Trip to Weston-Super-Mare	"	7.30 a.m.
Tue	"	10	" " " Barmouth	"	7.30 a.m.
Wed	"	11	" " " Skegness	"	7.30 a.m.
Thur	"	12	" " " New Brighton via the Mersey Tunnel	"	7.30 a.m.

Friday Saturday and Sunday—reserved

Mon	Sept	16	Day Trip to Rhyl	"	7.30 a.m.
Tue	"	17	" " " Southport	"	7.30 a.m.
Wed	"	18	" " " Weston-Super-Mare	"	7.30 a.m.

Saturday and Sunday—reserved

| Wed | Sept | 25 | Day Trip to Colwyn Bay | " | 7.30 a.m. |
| Sun | " | 29 | " " " Rhyl | " | 7.30 a.m. |

Seats may be reserved at any of our Agents.
Pensom's Stores, 6 Bordesley Green Road.
Hart's Stores, 1110 Stratford Road, Hall Green.
Bennett's Stores, 4 Gospel Farm Road, Hall Green.
Shirley Library, (next to Odeon) Stratford Road, Shirley.
or at Head Office.
Passengers may also board the Coaches at any of these points by appointment.

THE AVON PRESS, 148/150 STRATFORD ROAD, SPARKBROOK, BIRMINGHAM.

An early 1950's leaflet advertising day trips for August and September.

1952 – MOC 707 one of two rear-engined Foden PVRE6 "Landmaster" chassis with Bellhouse Hartwell 41 seat bodies purchased.

1954 – OOC 100, OOC 200, OOC 300 – three Daimler CVD6 with Burlingham "Seagull" 35 seat bodies. W.S.L. and W.G. Smith are seen collecting these vehicles from Daimler Motors representative.

1955 – RHP 774 a Daimler D65OHS "Freeline" chassis with attractive Duple "Elizabethan" 41 seat body.

Prior to entering service with Smiths this vehicle was used by Daimler as a demonstrator.

1957 – UOP 900 a Bedford SBG chassis with Duple "Vega" 41 seat body.
1958 – VOP 700 a further example was added - unfortunately no pictures exist.

From 1957 to 1964 Smiths purchased 14 Bedford SB chassis with Duple "Vega" and "Super Vega" bodywork making the whole fleet the same make.

A June 1959 view of 180 – 182 Stratford Road showing the new garage building and with the two Foden "Landmasters" MOC 707 and MOC 777 parked on the forecourt.

Day Tours to the Country

Tour No.

1 **ALDERSHOT.**—Stratford, Oxford, Wallingford, Pangbourne, Reading, Farnborough, Aldershot, Sandhurst, Wokingham, Henley-on-Thames, Oxford, Banbury, Warwick. A beautiful tour into the picturesque wooded area of Hampshire.

2 **BETTWS-Y-COED.**—Wolverhampton, Wellington, Shrewsbury and Llangollen. This tourist centre for Snowdonia is situated at the head of the wooded Vale of Conway, where the lovely Llugwy River joins the Conway River. The Swallow Falls and Fairy Glen are beauty spots to delight the eye of any visitor.

3 **BALA LAKES.**—Wolverhampton, Wellington and Shrewsbury into the Vale of Llangollen, where the Dee winds silver through wooded slopes and green hills. Then on to Corwen, lying under the shadow of the purple Berwyns. Twenty-two miles from here lies Bala Lake, truly a place of peace and tranquility.

4 **BATH AND WELLS.**—Alcester, Evesham, Cheltenham and Stroud into Somerset, where we meet the majestic Mendip Hills. Passing through Bath, with its eighteenth century architecture, we find scenes of unsurpassing beauty. Bath possesses the only hot springs in Britain, and by reason of its radio active waters is a renowned centre of healing. From here we proceed to Wells, a lovely and quiet Cathedral city, lying at the foot of the Mendips. Happily this city escaped war damage and is still the greatest monument of the middle ages we possess. Cheddar, curled up and snuggling against the mighty cliffs, is our next port of call, and the Gorge, which cuts the Mendip Hills in twain, provides some of the finest cliff scenery in Britain. From Cheddar we return through Axbridge, Bristol, Gloucester and Tewkesbury, through endless beauty spots and places of interest.

5 **BILLING AQUADROME.**—Coventry and Northampton. This beautiful 100-acre estate provides most of the amenities of the seaside combined with the delights of the country.

6 **CAMBRIDGE.**—Coventry, Daventry, Northampton, Bedford, St. Neots, Cambridge. Essentially a university town. Cambridge offers many attractions for the visitor, notably its fine buildings with their antiquity and architectural beauty. Returning via Huntingdon, Frapston, Kettering, Market Harborough, Rugby, Coventry.

7 **CHEDDAR.**—Worcester, Tewkesbury, Gloucester, Bristol. World famous for its magnificent Gorge, this picturesque little village lies at the foot of the Mendip Hills, and is overshadowed by majestic cliffs, which rise in places to a height of nearly 500 feet. Visitors will be enraptured by the magnificent spectacles that are to be seen in the various chambers of the Cheddar Caves.

8 **CHESTER.**—Wolverhampton, Newport, Whitchurch, Chester. The Cathedral walls, ancient timbered buildings, fine shops and beautiful River Dee are an unfailing source of interest to visitors. Returning via Wrexham, Ellesmere Lakes, Shrewsbury, Much Wenlock, Bridgnorth, Stourbridge.

9 **COTSWOLDS.**—Stratford, Moreton-in-the-Marsh, Stow-on-the-Wold, Bourton-on-the-Water, Northleach, Cirencester, Bibury, Burford, Chipping Norton, Long Compton, Shipston-on-Stour, Stratford. One of the most popular tours in this brochure, visitors are enthralled by the unrivalled scenery and honey-coloured stone buildings.

FROM BREEDON HILL   Photo: *Birmingham Post and Mail*

10 **CRANHAM WOODS.**—Evesham, Cheltenham, Birdlip, Cranham Woods, Gloucester, Tewkesbury, Worcester, Bromsgrove. At the western end of the Cotswold Hills the scenery here is thickly wooded.

11 **ELAN VALLEY.**—Worcester, Tenbury Wells, Leominster, Kington, New Radnor, Rhayader, through beautiful undulating scenery, of wooded and pasture land to the source of Birmingham's water supply. Great walls of water falling from the top of the dams to the river below are a vista of man's achievement. A chain of lakes, some natural and some caused by the flooding of the valleys, have made of the countryside a very picturesque Welsh lake district. We return via Llandrindod Wells, Bromyard and Worcester.

ELAN VALLEY WATERWORKS   Photo: *Birmingham Post and Mail*

IT'S NOT THE HOURS YOU PUT IN—BUT WHAT YOU PUT INTO THE HOURS

5

During the 1950's a series of brochures titled "By Road" were produced. These had suggested itineraries for private party customers and advertised some of the other services available from the company.

1959 – XOV 500 a Bedford SB3 chassis with 41 seat Duple "Vega" body.

An interior view of one of the Duple "Vega" bodied coaches – complete with traditional plastic headrest covers!

Part of the fleet lined-up for the camera at "The Regency Club" in Shirley – 1961.

Driver Peter Flannery.   Driver Frank Reynolds and W.G. Smith.

Drivers Bert Morton and John Rowlands.

Driver Reg Morgan.

1962 Deliveries 100, 200 and 300 FON - Bedford SB5's 41 seater Duple Super Vega's.
Left – Driver Frank Reynolds. Right – Driver Spencer Evans who also acted as Smiths carpenter!

Bedford SB – Duple "Super Vega", 222 DOJ waits for passengers arriving from the Isle of Wight at Southampton's Royal Pier in 1961.

The "Smiths Imperial Coaches" and map of Great Britain logo on the boot door was designed by W. G. Smith and was introduced in the late 1940's - it remained the same until 2001. This and the immaculate ivory and black livery made Smith's vehicles instantly recognisable.

The drivers and office staff all dressed up for a visit to the Motor Show at Earls Court in 1960.

Enjoying a meal on return from the show.

Some Tours for the Older Person

1962

ITINERARIES OF 8-DAY TOURS FOR EARLY AND LATE SEASON HOLIDAYS

BOURNEMOUTH, DORSET & THE ISLE OF WIGHT

First Day   To Bournemouth via the Cotswolds.
Second Day   At ease in Bournemouth.
Third Day   After lunch tour to Beaulieu Abbey & Lyndhurst.
Fourth Day   Day Tour to Isle of Wight with lunch at Ventnor.
Fifth Day   After lunch tour to Swanage & Corfe Castle.
Sixth Day   Day Tour to Weymouth and Portland Bill.
Seventh Day   At ease in Bournemouth.
Eighth Day   Return to Birmingham.

NEWQUAY, CORNWALL

First Day   To Newquay.
Second Day   After lunch tour to St. Mawes.
Third Day   After lunch tour to St. Austel and Mevagissey.
Fourth Day   Day Tour to St. Ives and Lands End.
Fifth Day   At ease.
Sixth Day   Day Tour to Truro and Falmouth.
Seventh Day   At ease.
Eighth Day   Return to Birmingham.
High Tea provided on return journey.

(Continued on page four)

SMITHS
IMPERIAL COACHES
LIMITED

HEAD OFFICE AND COACH STATION:
**180-182 STRATFORD ROAD,
BIRMINGHAM 11**
Telephone: VICtoria 2957-8-9 (Three Lines)

ILFRACOMBE

First Day   To Ilfracombe.
Second Day   At ease in Ilfracombe.
Third Day   After lunch tour to Woolacombe and Croyd Bay.
Fourth Day   Day Tour to Bude and Clovelly.
Fifth Day   After lunch tour to Barnstable, South Molton and Blackmore Gate.
Sixth Day   Day Tour to Doone Valley, Watersmeet, Valley of rocks and Lynmouth.
Seventh Day   At ease in Ilfracombe.
Eighth Day   Return to Birmingham.
Luncheon provided en-route on outward and return journey.

EXMOUTH AND DEVON

First Day   To Exmouth.
Second Day   Evening Circular Tour.
Third Day   After lunch tour to Sidmouth and Seaton.
Fourth Day   Day Tour to Looe.
Fifth Day   At ease in Exmouth.
Sixth Day   Day Tour to Buckfast Abbey and Torquay.
Seventh Day   Evening Circular Tour.
Eighth Day   Return to Birmingham.
Luncheon provided on outward and return journey.

WEYMOUTH AND DORSET

First Day   To Weymouth.
Second Day   Visit to Portland Bill.
Third Day   After lunch tour to Bridport and West Bay.
Fourth Day   Day Tour to Bournemouth and New Forest.
Fifth Day   At ease in Weymouth.
Sixth Day   Day tour to Lulworth Cove and Swanage.
Seventh Day   At ease in Weymouth.
Eighth Day   Return to Birmingham.

TORQUAY AND PAIGNTON

First Day   To Torquay.
Second Day   At ease in Torquay.
Third Day   After lunch tour to Paignton and Brixham.
Fourth Day   Day Tour to Dawlish, Exmouth and Sidmouth.
Fifth Day   At ease in Torquay.
Sixth Day   Day Tour to Buckfast Abbey and Dartmoor.
Seventh Day   After lunch visit to Cockington Forge.
Eighth Day   Return to Birmingham.
Luncheon provided on outward and return journey.

VENTNOR, Isle of Wight

First Day   To Southampton and steamer to Isle of Wight.
Second Day   At ease in Ventnor
Third Day   Half-day in Shanklin.
Fourth Day   After lunch tour to Brading Down and Bembridge.
Fifth Day   Day Tour to Ryde.
Sixth Day   Half-day in Sandown.
Seventh Day   After lunch tour to Carisbrook Castle, Yarmouth and The Needles.
Eighth Day   Return to Birmingham.
Luncheon provided on outward journey.

FARES AND DEPARTURE DATES ON REQUEST

"IT'S A PLEASURE - IT'S SMITHS"

1962 brochure of "Tours for the older person".

During 1962 the adjacent land and shops in Farm Road was acquired. The shops were later demolished to allow for a larger car parking area.

Some of the drivers and office staff with the 1898 Star: Bert Morton, John Rowlands, Frank Reynolds, "Bunny" Austin, Jean, Horace Tucker and Peter Flannery. Horace Tucker was the Garage Foreman and metal worker who was responsible for creating the panels on the vehicles built by Smiths.

The last days of the old house known as "Priorsleigh"...

...It was demolished during 1962 to make way for an extension of the garage and a proposed new office building.

A temporary office building was erected in 1962 – later extended, it served as the booking office until 2001!

A 1964 view of the extended garage building – the proposed new offices were never built.

1963 – 333 JOH a Bedford SB5 chassis with Duple's latest "Bella Vega" body seating 41.

Rear and offside views of 333 JOH prior to entering service.

1964 – 444 MOH another Duple "Bella Vega" bodied Bedford SB5 just being delivered to Stratford Rd.

This one had different side mouldings and a neater boot lid panel than that of the 1963 version.

Smiths forecourt also had a retail petrol station.

In 1964 a new sales kiosk was installed – quite different from today's petrol stations!

1964 – Petrol sales attendant, Peter Atkins, poses for the camera dressed-up in his "Beatles" suite.

"Over 50's" holiday-makers on tour in Bournemouth with Bert Morton driving 444 MOH.

1965 – COP 500C and COP 600C two Bedford VAL14 chassis' with Plaxton "Panorama" 52 seat bodies.

COP 500C – Stops in Robin Hood Lane, Hall Green.

COP 500C outside 45 Robin Hood Lane – The home of W.S.L. Smith.

Interior of COP 500C.

1966 – GOA 100D another Bedford VAL 14 chassis with Plaxton "Panorama" 52 seat body was added to the fleet.

A 1966 view of the garage with COP 500C, COP 600C and GOA 100D.

A bar was installed into one of the 1965 Bedford VALs for a special contract for Girling transporting their guests from Russia.

The bar top had a red covering – of course!

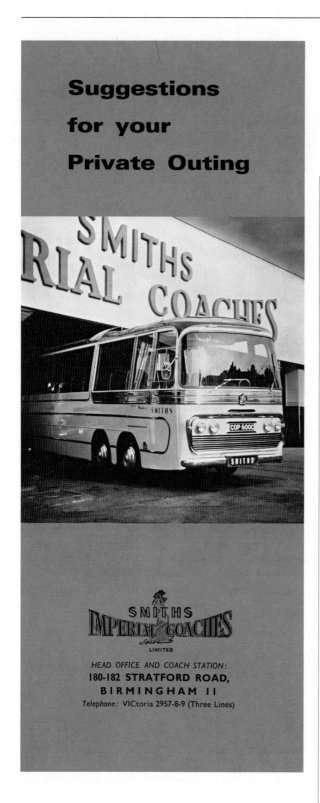

Suggestions

for your

Private Outing

LIMITED

HEAD OFFICE AND COACH STATION:

180-182 STRATFORD ROAD,

BIRMINGHAM 11

Telephone: VICtoria 2957-8-9 (Three Lines)

LIMITED

HEAD OFFICE AND COACH STATION:

180-182 STRATFORD ROAD,

BIRMINGHAM 11

Telephone: VIC 2957-8-9 (Three Lines)

Day Tours to the Seaside

ABERDOVEY.—Wolverhampton, Wellington, Shrewsbury, Welshpool and Newtown. The route lies through typical Welsh mountain scenery and terminates at a small picturesque town on the estuary of the River Dovey.

ABERYSTWYTH.—Kidderminster, Bewdley, Tenbury, Leominster, New Radnor, Llangurig and the towering masses of the Plynlimon Range, which shelter this popular resort, returning via Machynlleth, Newtown, Welshpool, Shrewsbury, Wolverhampton.

BANGOR—Isle of Anglesey.—Wolverhampton, Wellington, Shrewsbury, Llangollen, Bettws-y-Coed, Capel Curig to the gateway to the Isle of Anglesey, an ancient and historic city.

BARMOUTH.—Wolverhampton, Wellington, Shrewsbury, Welshpool, Dolgelley. This town, set in wonderful mountain scenery, lies at the mouth of the River Mawddach and has a firm sandy beach.

BARRY ISLAND.—Worcester, Ross-on-Wye, Monmouth, Newport and Cardiff. A beautiful journey through the Wye Valley, terminated at a place ideally suited to young children. One beach of fine sand and another of pebbles, both excellent for bathing. Return via M.5.

BLACKPOOL, via M.6 to Preston. Famous for its beach, its invigorating air and its entertainments.

BOGNOR REGIS.—Stratford, Oxford, Newbury, Winchester, Bognor Regis. Facing south on the smiling Sussex coast Bognor Regis has everything that a family requires for a happy and successful visit.

BOURNEMOUTH, via Stratford, Moreton-in-the-Marsh, Stow-on-the-Wold, Burford, Swindon, Marlborough and Salisbury, and returning the reverse route. A journey over the Cotswolds to a lovely garden town.

BRIDPORT AND WEST BAY.—Stratford, Stow-on-the-Wold, Burford, Marlborough, Salisbury, Blandford, Bridport and West Bay. West Bay is a secluded Dorset fishing village set in beautiful countryside, so closely associated with Thomas Hardy's "Wessex Novels".

BRIGHTON.—Motorway M.1. London, Horsham, Henfield, Brighton. Golden beaches and the splendours of Regency Architecture. See the fantastic Royal Pavilion and the 18th century bow-fronted curio shops. Brighton is the home of many film, stage and T.V. personalities.

"IT'S A PLEASURE - IT'S SMITHS"

A 1960's version of the private party organiser's book.

1967 – JOF 800E and JOE 900E two Bedford VAM5 chassis with Duple "Bella Venture" 45 seat bodies.

JOF 800E and JOE 900E on the Stratford Road forecourt.

1967 – JOV 700E another Bedford VAM5 chassis added to the fleet, this time with Duple "Viceroy" 45 seat body.

Front and rear views of JOV 700E.

```
        SMITHS  IMPERIAL  COACHES LTD.              SUNDAY     - AUGUST  4th
        180 Stratford Road, B'ham 11.        B Southsea (Navy Days)         23/6d
            Phone:-VIC 2957-8-9              B Bournemouth                  25/-d
               Programme for                * Weymouth                      27/-d
         July 29th to August 10th           B Weston-super-Mare            20/-d
                                            B Beaulieu Abbey & New Forest  23/6d
       Tours marked * start at 7-00am.          MONDAY     - AUGUST  5th
            MONDAY   - JULY 29th            B Bournemouth                  25/-d
   B Bournemouth              18/6d         B Richmond & Hampton Court     23/6d
   A Rhyl                     15/-d         A Skegness                     23/6d
   A Porthcawl                17/6d         B Southsea(Navy Days)          23/6d
   C Woburn Abbey & Zoo Park  14/-d             TUESDAY    - AUGUST  6th
   E Alton Towers              9/-d         A Morecambe                    24/-d
            TUESDAY  - JULY 30th            B Southsea (Navy Days)         23/6d
   A Aberystwyth              15/6d         A Aberystwyth                  21/-d
   A Morecambe                18/-d         B Cheddar & The Mendip Hills   21/-d
   B Southsea                 17/6d         A Rhyl                         20/-d
   D Wicksteed Park           11/-d            WEDNESDAY - AUGUST  7th
   F Bourton-on-the-Water     10/-d         B Kew Gardens(LONDON)10hrs.stay 14/-d
            WEDNESDAY - JULY 31st           B Weston-super-Mare            15/-d
   GUERNSEY, Channel Isles    56/-d         A Porthcawl                    17/6d
   B Kew Gardens(LONDON)10hrs. stay 14/-d   B London Airport Tour          18/-d
   B Weston-super-Mare        15/-d         E Dovedale                     10/-d
   C The Peaks & Chatsworth Hse. 12/6d         THURSDAY  - AUGUST  8th
   E Bridgnorth Circular Tour  7/-d         A Llandudno & Rhyl    16/6d &  15/-d
            THURSDAY - AUGUST  1st          B Windsor & River Cruise       18/-d
   A Llandudno & Rhyl   16/6d & 15/-d       B Isle of Wight                24/-d
   * Weymouth                 20/3d         C Woburn Abbey & Zoo Park      14/-d
   D Oxford & River Cruise    19/-d         E Trentham Gardens              9/-d
   E Ludlow & Clee Hills       8/6d             FRIDAY    - AUGUST  9th
            FRIDAY   - AUGUST  2nd          B Weston-super-Mare            15/-d
   B Bournemouth              18/6d         B Bournemouth                  18/6d
   B Weston-super-Mare        15/-d         A Barmouth                     15/6d
   B Windsor & River Cruise   18/-d         C The Peaks & Haddon Hall      12/6d
   C Whipsnade Zoo            14/-d         F Broadway & Evesham            7/6d
   F Malvern Hills             8/9d
```

A mid 1960's day trip leaflet.

1969 – ROB 200G and ROB 300G two new Bedford VAM70 chassis with the latest style of Duple's Viceroy body seating 45.

Both coaches were originally delivered in 'Brilliant White' but were immediately sent back to Duple for a repaint!

ROB 300G – Parked at a day excursion destination.

1970 – UOL 400H a Bedford VAL 70 chassis with Plaxton "Panorama Elite" 53 seat body.

1970 – Another view of UOL 400H on delivery day from Plaxtons. Note the trade plates visible in the windscreen.

1970 - Coaches arriving at the Civic Hall in Solihull for the annual "Over 50's" Concert and Holiday Programme launch.

444 MOH on duty.

These popular events always "sold-out" and allowed those attending first viewing of the new season's holiday programme.

Refreshments and entertainment were included in the evening's programme with stars such as Don Maclean making an appearance on more than one occasion.

SMITHS IMPERIAL COACHES LTD.
180-182 STRATFORD ROAD, BIRMINGHAM 11
Telephone: 772-2957-8-9

SUMMER HOLIDAY EXPRESS SERVICES

BOURNEMOUTH
Outward every Saturday from last Saturday in May

		OUTWARD	RETURN
Erdington	STOCKLAND GARAGE	*dep.* 6–10 a.m.	*arr.* 8–39 a.m.
Washwood Heath	FOX AND GOOSE HOTEL	6–25	8–29
Yardley	BULLS HEAD, COVENTRY ROAD	6–30	8–19
Sparkbrook	COACH STATION	7–00	8–09
Hall Green	ROBIN HOOD HOTEL	7–08	8–01
Shirley	ODEON CINEMA	7–11	7–57
Solihull	BARLEY MOW	7–16	7–52
Bournemouth	GLEN FERN CAR PARK	*arr.* 1–09 p.m.	*dep.* 2–00 p.m.

RETURN FARE £2.85

WEYMOUTH
Outward every Saturday from first Saturday in July

		OUTWARD	RETURN
Erdington	STOCKLAND GARAGE	*dep.* 6–10 a.m.	*arr.* 9–11 p.m.
Washwood Heath	FOX AND GOOSE HOTEL	6–25	8–56
Yardley	BULLS HEAD, COVENTRY ROAD	6–30	8–46
Sparkbrook	COACH STATION	7–00	8–36
Hall Green	ROBIN HOOD HOTEL	7–08	8–28
Shirley	ODEON CINEMA	7–11	8–24
Solihull	BARLEY MOW	7–16	8–19
Hockley Heath	NAGS HEAD	7–28	8–06
Henley-in-Arden	HENLEY MEMORIAL	7–33	8–01
Weymouth	SIDNEY HALL	*arr.* 1–30 p.m.	*dep.* 2–00 p.m.

RETURN FARE £3.05

SOUTH DEVON (Seaton, Sidmouth, Exmouth)
Outward every Friday from Second Week in June

		OUTWARD	RETURN
Erdington	STOCKLAND GARAGE	*dep.* 11–10 p.m.	*arr.* 7–05 p.m.
Washwood Heath	FOX AND GOOSE HOTEL	11–25	6–55
Yardley	BULLS HEAD, COVENTRY ROAD	11–30	6–45
Sparkbrook	COACH STATION	12 Mdnt.	6–35
Hall Green	ROBIN HOOD HOTEL	12–09 a.m.	6–26
Shirley	ODEON CINEMA	12–13	6–22
Solihull	BARLEY MOW	12–29	6–15
Lyme Regis		*arr.* 7–30	
Seaton	STATION ROAD	*arr.* 8–03	*dep.* 10–32 a.m.
Sidmouth	MUNICIPAL CAR PARK	*arr.* 8–25	*dep.* 10–10 a.m.
Exmouth	MORTON ROAD	*arr.* 9–03	*dep.* 9–33 a.m.

RETURN FARES: SEATON £3.40 – SIDMOUTH £3.80 – EXMOUTH £3.95

LOOE (Cornwall)
Outward every Friday from first Friday in July

		OUTWARD	RETURN
Erdington	STOCKLAND GARAGE	*dep.* 11–10 p.m.	*arr.* 8–47 p.m.
Washwood Heath	FOX AND GOOSE HOTEL	11–25	8–33
Yardley	BULLS HEAD, COVENTRY ROAD	11–30	8–24
Sparkbrook	COACH STATION	12 Mdnt.	8–12
Hall Green	ROBIN HOOD HOTEL	12–05 a.m.	8–02
Shirley	ODEON CINEMA	12–09	7–59
East Looe	QUAY CAR PARK	*arr.* 9–14	*dep.* 10–30 a.m.

RETURN FARE £4.90

NEWQUAY (Cornwall)
OPERATED BY STOCKLAND GARAGE LTD.
Outward every Friday from first week in July

		OUTWARD
Erdington	STOCKLAND GARAGE	*dep.* 11–00 p.m.
Yardley	SWAN HOTEL	11–25 p.m.
Sparkbrook	SMITHS COACH STATION	11–35 p.m.
Newquay	MANOR CAR PARK	*dep.* 10–00 a.m. Sat.

RETURN FARE £5.50 (*No Deposits on this Service*)

A DEPOSIT WILL SECURE YOUR SEATS UNTIL 28 DAYS BEFORE DAY OF TRAVEL (MIN. £1.00 PER SEAT)

PUSH CHAIRS AND ANIMALS CANNOT BE CARRIED ON THESE SERVICES

Cancellations cannot be accepted after 28 days before date of departure. Cancellations received after this day will be offered for sale and refunds made accordingly. There will be a 10% booking charge on all cancellations.

Accommodation available at all these resorts—see separate leaflet for details.

Saturday express services were operated throughout the summer months. This leaflet advertises the destinations available for 1971.

TOURS FOR THE OVER 50's

BOOK AT

LIMITED

180-182 Stratford Rd., Sparkbrook, Birmingham B11 1AQ

Telephone: 021-772 2957

OR THEIR AGENTS

Second issue 1972

The 1972 brochure of "Over 50's" holidays.

1972

BOURNEMOUTH & LYMINGTON
Outward every Saturday from the last Saturday in May

		outward	return
Erdington	Stockland Garage	dep.0610	arr.2042
Washwood Heath	Fox & Goose Hotel..	" 0625	" 2032
Yardley	Bulls Head, Coventry Road	" 0630	" 2027
Sparkbrook	Smiths Imperial Coach Station... ..	" 0700	" 2012
Hall Green	Robin Hood Island..	" 0708	" 2004
Shirley	Odeon Cinema..	" 0711	" 2001
Solihull	Barley Mow Hotel	" 0716	" 1956
LYMINGTON	Pier..	arr.1221	dep.1451
BOURNEMOUTH	Glen Fern Car Park.	arr.1306	" 1400

		Adults	Children
Return Fares	BOURNEMOUTH	£3.55	£2.35
	LYMINGTON	£3.40	£2.30

WEYMOUTH
Outward every Saturday from the first Saturday in July

		outward	return
Erdington	Stockland Garage	dep.0610	arr.2111
Washwood Heath	Fox & Goose Hotel..	" 0625	" 2056
Yardley	Bulls Head, Coventry Road	" 0630	" 2046
Sparkbrook	Smiths Imperial Coach Station.. .. ..."	0700	" 2036
Hall Green	Robin Hood Island..	" 0708	" 2028
Shirley	Odeon Cinema	" 0711	" 2024
Solihull	Barley Mow Hotel	" 0716	" 2019
Hockley Heath	The Wayfarer	" 0728	" 2006
Henley In Arden	Memorial Cross	" 0733	" 2001
WEYMOUTH	Preston Road Car Park.	arr.1330	dep 1400

	Adults	Children
Return Fares	£3.70	£2.50

LOOE (Cornwall)
Outward Fridays of Main Holiday Weeks in July.

		outward	return
Erdington	Stockland Garage	dep.2310	arr.2047
Washwood Heath	Fox & Goose Hotel..	" 2325	" 2033
Yardley	Bulls Head	" 2330	" 2024
Sparkbrook	Smiths Imperial Coach Station	" mdnt	" 2012
Hall Green	Robin Hood Island..	" 0005	" 2002
Shirley	Odeon Cinema	" 0009	" 1959
EAST LOOE	Quay Car Park.	arr.0914	dep.1030

	Adults	Children
Return Fares	£5.25	£3.50

A NEW SERVICE to the Isle of Wight with through bookings to
SANDOWN, SHANKLIN & VENTNOR via SOUTHAMPTON.
Outward every Saturday from the last Saturday in May.

		outward	return
Erdington	Stockland Garage..	dep.0610	arr.2042
Washwood Heath	Fox & Goose Hotel	" 0625	" 2032
Yardley	Bulls Head, Coventry Road. ..	" 0630	" 2027
Sparkbrook	Smiths Imperial Coach Station	" 0700	" 2012
Hall Green	Robin Hood Island	" 0708	" 2004
Shirley	Odeon Cinema..	" 0711	" 2001
Solihull	Barley Mow Hotel.	" 0716	" 1956
SOUTHAMPTON	Royal Pier	arr 1136	dep.1536
	Red Funnel Steamer . .. ..departs 1230		
EAST COWES	Trinity Wharf	arr.1340	dep.1415
SANDOWN	Fort Street	" 1425	" 1330*
SHANKLIN	Bus Station	" 1435	" 1330*
VENTNOR	Pier Street Coach Station. ..	" 1450	" 1315*

* The return times from the Island's resorts are the latest times *
permissable in order to connect with Steamer Earlier coaches do run.

Return fares		Adults	Children
including	SOUTHAMPTON only	£3.40	£2.30
Steamer &	EAST COWES	£4.40	£3.00
Southern	SANDOWN	£5.10	£3.40
Vectis Coach	SHANKLIN	£5.10	£3.40
	VENTNOR	£5.10	£3.40

SEATON, SIDMOUTH & EXMOUTH (South Devon)
Outward every Friday from second Friday in June (return Saturday)

		outward	return
Erdington	Stockland Garage.. .. ..dep.2310		arr. 1905
Washwood Heath	fox & Goose Hotel.	" 2325	" 1855
Yardley	Bulls Head, Coventry Road.. ..	" 2330	" 1845
Sparkbrook	Smiths imperial coach Stn.. ..	" mdnt	" 1835
Hall Green	Robin Hood Island.	" 0009	" 1826
Shirley	Odeon Cinema..	" 0013	" 1822
Solihull	Barley Mow Hotel.	" 0029	" 1815
SEATON	Station Road.. .. ..arr 0803		dep. 1032
SIDMOUTH	Municipal Car Park..	" 0825	" 1010
EXMOUTH	Morton Road	" 0903	" 0930

		Adults	Children
Return Fares	SEATON	£3.85	£2.55
	SIDMOUTH	£4.35	£2.90
	EXMOUTH	£4.45	£2.95

1972 summer express services.

1972 – DOE 111K another Bedford VAL70 chassis fitted with Plaxton "Panorama Elite II" 53 seat body. This was one of the last Bedford VAL chassis made and was sold to John Watson who occasionally drove for Smiths.

DOE 111K in its later "Watsonians" livery which was occasionally used by Smiths "on hire" from John Watson.

... Aug. ...

A	Llandudno	£1.15
A	Rhyl	£1.05
A	Hunstanton	£1.20
C	Woburn Abbey & Park	£0.85

FRIDAY Aug. 2nd

B	Weston	£1.05
B	Bournemouth	£1.25
B	Royal Windsor	£1.05
F	Evesham Circular	£0.65

SATURDAY Aug. 3rd

| D* | Bournemouth | £1.40 |
| B* | Weymouth | £1.40 |

SUNDAY Aug. 4th

B	Weston	£1.15
B	Bournemouth	£1.40
A	Rhyl	£1.15
A	Llandudno	£1.30
D	Forest of Dean	£0.95
E	Clee Hills & Ludlow	£0.70
G	Evening Tour	£0.40

MONDAY Aug. 5th

B	Weston	£1.05
B	Bournemouth	£1.25
B*	Exmouth Devon	£1.50
F	Broadway & Evesham	£0.60

TUESDAY Aug. 6th

B	Southsea	£1.25
A	Caernarvon	£1.35
B	Windsor Safari Park	£1.50
F	Symonds Yat	£0.70

WEDNESDAY Aug. 7th

B	Weston	£1.05
B*	Brighton	£1.40
B	Cheddar Caves	£1.10
F	Banbury Circular	£0.60

THURSDAY Aug. 8th

A	Llandudno	£1.15
A	Rhyl	£1.05
A	Chester Zoo	£0.95
B	Burnham-on-Sea	£1.20
F	Bourton-on-the-Water	£0.75

FRIDAY Aug. 9th

B	Weston	£1.05
B	Bournemouth	£1.25
A	Skegness	£1.25
F	Hereford Circular	£0.70

SATURDAY Aug. 10th

| A | Southend Illuminatns | £1.50 |
| D | London (Kew Gardens) | £1.25 |

SUNDAY Aug. 11th

B	Weston	£1.15
B	Bournemouth	£1.40
A	Lake Windermere incl Cruise on Lake	£1.85
A	Beaumaris - Anglesey	£1.40
D	Dovedale	£0.75
G	Evening Circular	£0.40

MONDAY Aug. 12th

B	Weston	£1.05
B	Bournemouth	£1.25
A	Barry Island	£1.15
C	Woburn House & Park	£0.85
F	Afternoon Circular	£0.40

TUESDAY Aug. 13th

B	Southsea	£1.25
B	Ryde, Isle of Wight	£2.00
D*	Teignmouth	£1.50
D	Slimbridge Wild Fowl Trust	£0.85
F	Cotswold Tour	£0.70

WEDNESDAY Aug.14th

B	Weston	£1.05
B	Royal Windsor	£1.05
A	Southend-on-Sea	£1.40
D	Oxford & Bleneim	£0.80
E	Clee Hills & Ludlow	£0.70

THURSDAY Aug 15th

A	Llandudno	£1.15
A	Rhyl	£1.05
A	Clacton-on-Sea	£1.40
B	Lions of Longleat	£1.60
E	Bridgnorth Circular	£0.60

FRIDAY Aug 16th

B	Weston	£1.05
B	Bournemouth	£1.25
A	Blackpool	£1.30
A	Southport Sands	£1.10
B	Bristol Zoo	£1.00

SATURDAY Aug. 17th

| B | London, Kew Gardens & Hampton Court | £1.35 |

SUNDAY Aug. 18th

B*	Sidmouth	£1.50
B	Bournemouth	£1.40
B	Weston	£1.15
B	Southsea	£1.40
F	Cotswold Tour	£0.75
G	Evening Tour	£0.40

MONDAY Aug. 19th

B	Weston	£1.05
B	Bournemouth	£1.25
A	Blackpool	£1.30
A	Rhyl	£1.05
E	Alton Towers	£0.70

TUESDAY Aug. 20th

B	Southsea	£1.25
B	Ryde - I.o.Wight	£2.00
A	Porthcawl	£1.30
D	Wye Valley	£1.05
E	Teme Valley	£0.60

WEDNESDAY Aug 21st

B	Weston	£1.05
A*	Scarborough	£1.50
A	Hunstanton	£1.20
C	The Peaks & Chatswth	£0.90
E	Matlock	£0.70

THURSDAY Aug 22nd

A	Llandudno	£1.15
A	Rhyl	£1.05
A	Aberystwyth	£1.15
D	Forest Of Dean	£0.95
F	Pershore & Evesham	£0.70

FRIDAY Aug 23rd

B	Weston	£1.05
B	Bournemouth	£1.25
B	Bristol Zoo	£1.00
B	Clevedon	£1.05

SATURDAY Aug. 24th

| C | Leeds v."Blues" | £1.25 |

SUNDAY Aug. 25th

B	Bournemouth	£1.40
B	Weston	£1.15
A	Lake Windermere incl. Cruise	£1.85
A	Blackpool	£1.40

MONDAY Aug. 26th

B	Weston	£1.25
B	Bournemouth	£1.50
A	Caernarvon	£1.45
B*	Weymouth	£1.50

TUESDAY Aug 27th

B	Southsea	£1.40
B	Bournemouth	£1.40
B	Weston	£1.15
B*	Teignmouth	£1.50
F	Symonds Yat	£0.70

WEDNESDAY Aug. 28th

B	Weston	£1.05
A	Morecambe	£1.40
A	Blackpool	£1.30
F	Broadway & Evesham	£0.60
-	Leicester v. Blues	£0.60

THURSDAY Aug. 29th

A	Llandudno	£1.15
A	Rhyl	£1.05
A	Chester Zoo	£0.95
B	Lions of Longleat	£1.60
F	Bourton-on-Water	£0.70

FRIDAY Aug. 30th

B	Weston	£1.05
B	Bournemouth	£1.25
B	Windsor & River C.	£1.75
F	Banbury Circular	£0.60

SUNDAY Aug 31st

B	Weston	£1.15
B	Bournemouth	£1.40
B	Hampton Court	£1.25
A	Llandudno via the Horseshoe Pass	£1.35

oooooooooooooooooooooooooooo
FOLLOW THE "BLUES" TO
ALL AWAY MATCHES WITH US
oooooooooooooooooooooooooooo

**B L A C K P O O L
I L L U M I N A T I O N S**

Sept. 6th to Oct. 27th

DAY EXCURSIONS

Mid-week.....£1.40
Saturdays....£1.65

TWO-DAY EXCURSIONS
Including Dinner, Bed and Breakfast

Mid-week.....£4.00
Weekend......£5.00

All excursions leave Birmingham at 7.45 a.m.

Day Tours return from Blackpool at 12 midnight

Two-day Tours return from Blackpool at 3.00 pm.

ooooooooooooooooo

* next to Starting time letter indicates that the starting time will be 45 MINUTES EARLIER.

ooooooooooooooooo

September & Winter Programme ready Aug. 7th

1974 – A typical day trip programme.

SMITHS IMPERIAL COACHES LTD
180,Stratford Rd. B'ham 11.
'phone 772-2957

HOLIDAY TOURS FOR THE OVER 50's, 1974

Date	Destination		Hotel	Inclusive Price
May 4th	SCARBOROUGH	& Yorkshire Moors	Delmont Hotel	£28.50
May 11th	SCARBOROUGH	& Yorkshire Moors	Delmont Hotel	£29.50
	SHANKLIN	& Isle of Wight	Bungalow Hotel	£35.00
	HASTINGS	& Sussex	Executive Hotel	£34.50
May 18th	HASTINGS	& Sussex	Executive Hotel	£35.50
May 25th	SCARBOROUGH	& Yorkshire Moors	Norbreck Hotel	£38.50
	NEWQUAY	& Cornwall	Sandy Lodge Hotel	£32.00
	DOLLAR	& Scotland	Dollarbeg Hotel	£38.50
June 1st	SHANKLIN	& Isle of Wight	Bungalow Hotel	£36.50
	NEWQUAY	& Cornwall	Sandy Lodge Hotel	£32.50
	MINEHEAD	& North Devon	Cresta Hotel	£32.00
	DOLLAR	& Scotland	Dollarbeg Hotel	£41.50
June 8th	MINEHEAD	& North Devon	Cresta Hotel	£32.50
	DOLLAR	& Scotland	Dollarbeg Hotel	£41.50
June 15th	FALMOUTH	& Cornwall	Membley Hall Hotel	£35.50
	MINEHEAD	& North Devon	Cresta Hotel	£33.50
June 29th	SHANKLIN	& Isle of Wight	Bungalow Hotel	£36.50
Aug. 25th	SHANKLIN	& Isle of Wight	Bungalow Hotel	£36.00
Aug 31st	NEWQUAY	& FALMOUTH	Membley Hall Hotel	£34.50
	SCARBOROUGH	& Yorkshire Moors	Norbreck Hotel	£38.50
Sept. 1st	SHANKLIN	& Isle of Wight	Bungalow Hotel	£35.50
	MINEHEAD	& North Devon	Cresta Hotel	£33.50
Sept 7th	SCARBOROUGH	& Yorkshire Moors	Norbreck Hotel	£38.00
	NEWQUAY	& Cornwall	Sandy Lodge Hotel	£31.50
	HASTINGS	& Sussex	Executive Hotel	£36.50
Sept 8th	MINEHEAD	& North Devon	Cresta Hotel	£32.50
Sept 14th	SCARBOROUGH	& Yorkshire Moors	Delmont Hotel	£32.00
	NEWQUAY	& FALMOUTH	Membley Hall Hotel	£32.50
	DUNOON	& Scotland	Cowal House Hotel	£39.00
Sept.15th	SHANKLIN	& Isle of Wight	Bungalow Hotel	£32.50
	MINEHEAD	& North Devon	Cresta Hotel	£32.00
Sept.21st	NEWQUAY	& Falmouth	Membley Hall Hotel	£32.50
	DUNOON	& Scotland	Cowal House Hotel	£36.50
Sept 22nd	SHANKLIN	& Isle of Wight	Bungalow Hotel	£32.50
	MINEHEAD	& North Devon	Cresta Hotel	£31.50
Sept 28th	HASTINGS	& Sussex	Executive Hotel	£33.50
	NEWQUAY	& Falmouth	Membley Hall Hotel	£32.00
Sept.29th	SHANKLIN	& Isle of Wight	Bungalow Hotel	£31.50
	MINEHEAD	& North Devon	Cresta Hotel	£31.00
Oct 6th	SHANKLIN	& Isle of Wight	Bungalow Hotel	£31.00

A SMALL DEPOSIT WILL SECURE YOUR RESERVATION.

1974 Holiday price list which accompanied a colour leaflet.

Roger Smith takes delivery of two new Bedford YRT chassis with Plaxton "Panorama Elite III" 53 seat bodies from Plaxton's representative at the Scarborough factory.

Both vehicles, ROX 800M and ROX 900M had a gold stripe and commemorative lettering added to the livery to celebrate the company's "Golden Jubilee" year in 1974.

The gold stripe and special lettering were later deleted to revert to the standard livery.

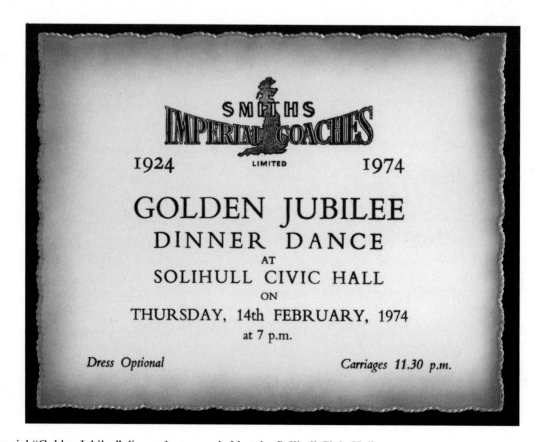

A special "Golden Jubilee" dinner-dance was held at the Solihull Civic Hall.

Smiths stand at the 3rd International Holiday Exhibition which was held at Bingley Hall between December 29th 1975 and January 20th 1976.

Official passes from the International Holiday Exhibition.

An aerial view of Sparkbrook and the surrounding area, taken early 1976 with Smiths garage to the right of the picture, circled white.

1976 – LDA 500P a new Bedford YRT chassis with Duple "Dominant" 53 seat body. This was the last of many Bedford vehicles purchased.

During its last years of service with Smiths its "466" engine was replaced in-house by a "500 turbo" unit. It is still currently in service in Birmingham with Meadway Coaches.

NWD 755P another new vehicle added to the fleet for 1976, a Ford R1114 chassis with 53 seat body by Van-Hool, it was the first Ford operated.

Added to the fleet during May 1976, due to exceptional demand, this vehicle was purchased and in service within one week!

1977 version of the "Over 50's" holiday brochure –
red, white and blue for the Queen's silver jubilee year!

1977 Publicity Coach.

During January 1977 special permission was granted to park a publicity coach on Temple Row behind
"Rackhams" store.

1977 – RDA 100R a Ford R1114 chassis with Plaxton "Supreme" 53 seat body. The garage doors were re-painted blue and white with a red stripe for the Queen's Silver Jubilee year – silver crowns were also applied on the red band - they can just be seen in the picture.

Front and Rear of RDA 100R, the logo never changed.

Passports bid to defeat hooligans

by ROBERT MOORE

ANTI-HOOLIGAN passports for soccer fans are being issued by one of Birmingham's biggest coach firms.

Without one, even pensioners cannot travel on Smith's Imperial Coaches to Blues or Villa away matches.

Birmingham City fans on coaches to Everton had to show their passports for the first time today.

The scheme is "the last desperate throw" by Smith's general manager, Mr. Norman Taylor, who is fed up with his coaches being wrecked by soccer vandals.

"It had better work," he said· "If it does not, we will stop soccer coaches altogether."

DUPLICATES

Smith's have had thousands of the passports printed.

Supporters obtain duplicate cards from the firm's offices in Stratford Road and then stick on two passport-size pictures of themselves.

They must get a church minister, doctor, schoolmaster or their employer to sign the passport.

The wording above the signature says: "I certify that to the best of my knowledge the above mentioned is a responsible citizen and is unlikely to indulge in bad behaviour at, en-route to, or from football matches."

Mr. Norman Taylor, general manager of Smith's Imperial Coaches, with some of the anti-hooligan passports.

An example of the anti-hooligan passports for travelling soccer fans.

For many years coaches were operated to the away matches of Birmingham City F.C. and Aston Villa. After experiencing vandalism to their vehicles Smiths introduced special passports for the passengers who travelled to these events.

The introduction of these caused interest in the local press and the General Manager, Norman Taylor was interviewed on local ITV news.

1978 view of the garage and booking office.

Another view of the garage also taken in 1978.

1978 – VJW 600S and VJW 700S two Ford R1114 chassis with Duple Dominant II 53 seat bodies.

VJW 600S outside the garage.

VJW 600S and VJW 700S outside the garage.

VJW 600S was photographed without number plates for publicity pictures.

Top - The "Over 50's" holiday brochure for 1978. Bottom - A special leaflet was issued for holidays to Guernsey and Jersey as well as the Summer Saturday express services.

1979 – XVP 300T an AEC Reliance chassis with Duple Dominant II 53 seat body.

1979 – XVP 300T was only the second AEC operated after KOB 100 in 1949.

XVP 300T was later given cherished number plate YAU 400 as seen in this photograph.

Smiths were enthusiastic supporters of the West Midlands Coach Rally that was held at the Goodyear factory in Wolverhampton. Their efforts were rewarded with various cups and awards.

Here at the 1980 rally driver Peter Flannery collects the Leyland Challenge and Arlington trophies from Ron Whittle.

Drivers and office staff with W.G. Smith celebrating the return from a staff holiday to Scotland.

"Better travel by Smiths"…This message was applied to the roofs of several coaches to advertise to the occupiers of high-rise buildings. LDA 500P is seen here aboard a Red Funnel Isle of Wight ferry.

Top - Space rocket luggage labels were produced to follow the theme of the brochure!

The cover for the 1980 holiday brochure had a futuristic theme and this was continued over to the introductory page… "Our other world impression overleaf does not appear as a holiday in this year's brochure – due to the shortage of space suits – but your grandchildren could be interested! We'll see what our brochure for the year 2,000 AD offers!"

1980 – FJW 400V a Leyland Leopard chassis with 57 seat Plaxton Supreme IV body. This coach served the company for over 20 years only being sold (for preservation) at the end of trading in 2001.

Front FJW 400V.   Rear FJW 400V.

During the winter months one of the coaches would have posters applied to the windows advertising the company's holidays, day trips and other services.

Here XVP 300T is parked in the Bull Ring with the driver distributing the 1981 brochure to potential customers.

The 1981 version of the "Over 50's" holiday brochure was A4 size for the first time.

1981 – KOF 444W the only mini coach ever operated, a Dodge 50 with 25 seat Reeve-Burgess body. Roger Smith models a "corporate" sweater – although this was not standard issue! The "I've got big brothers" slogan on the rear panel was a reminder that Smiths also operated 53 and 57 seat coaches.

More awards at the West Midlands Coach Rally, this time the Leyland and Keiko trophies for FJW 400V in 1982.

180-182 Stratford Rd., Birmingham, B11 1AQ. Tel: 021-772 2957

PROGRAMME FOR MARCH & APRIL 1983

SUPER DAY SHOPPING EXCURSIONS TO FRANCE

On Fridays the 4th and 25th March we depart Birmingham at 23.00 hrs for Dover, arriving early Saturday morning for the ferry to Calais. From Calais we proceed to the Hypermarket at Boulogne where you can experience duty free shopping "French Style". We then proceed to the town of Boulogne for some free time before returning to Calais. We expect to arrive back in Birmingham around mid-night.

COST

March 4th..........Adult £18   Child £12
March 25th.........Adult £20   Child £13.50
For British Citizens without passports we can arrange Identity Cards.

OUR OWN COACH TRAVELS OVER - VIA DOVER !

MOTHER'S DAY SPECIAL
SUNDAY MARCH 13th
A Day In
WESTON-SUPER-MARE
Including three course
lunch and coffee £7.50

SUNDAY MARCH 27th
A Day In
WESTON-SUPER-MARE
Start 07.45am Home for 9.00pm
£4.85

Day trip leaflets 1982 and 1983.

Norman Taylor, General Manager retired in 1984 after serving the company for more than 30 years. He is seen holding his newly issued bus pass.

SUNDAY SEPTEMBER 2nd		
Weston-super-Mare		£4.50
Teignmouth		£5.50
Alton Towers including		
admission and rides		£6.50
MONDAY SEPTEMBER 3rd		
Weston-super-Mare		£4.50
Burnham-on-Sea		£4.50
Blackpool "lights"		£5.00
TUESDAY SEPTEMBER 4th		
Portsmouth & Southsea		£5.30
Barry Island		£4.75
Moreton-in-Marsh Market		£3.00
WEDNESDAY SEPTEMBER 5th		
Weston-super-Mare		£4.50
Cheddar Caves		£4.50
Southampton and Solent		
Cruise to Isle of Wight		£8.00
THURSDAY SEPTEMBER 6th		
Rhyl		£3.60✓
International Garden Festival		
Liverpool inc.admission		£7.50*
Southport Sands		£4.85
Bourton-on-the-Water		£3.00
FRIDAY SEPTEMBER 7th		
Weston-super-Mare		£4.50
Bournemouth		£5.30
Afternoon Circular		£2.00
SUNDAY SEPTEMBER 9th		
"Emmerdale Farm Country"		
Inc.Guided tour and lunch		£12
Weston-super-Mare		£4.50
Farnborough Air Show		
(admission extra)		£5.50
Bewdley Safari Park		
Including admission		£4.00
MONDAY SEPTEMBER 10th		
Weston-super-Mare		£4.50
Clevedon		£4.50
Oxford & Thames Cruise		£5.00
TUESDAY SEPTEMBER 11th		
Blackpool (6 pm return)		£5.00
Rhyl		£4.60
Historical Chester		£4.00
Milton Keynes fabulous		
Shopping Centre		£3.50

	WEDNESDAY SEPTEMBER 12th	
B	Weston-super-Mare	£4.50
B	Southampton and Solent	
	Cruise to Isle of Wight	£8.00
F	Cotswolds Tour	£3.00
	THURSDAY SEPTEMBER 13th	
A	Rhyl	£4.60
A	Llandudno	£5.10
A	International Garden Festival	
	Liverpool.Inc.admission	£7.50
F	Blackpool "lights"	£5.00
	FRIDAY SEPTEMBER 14th	
B	Bournemouth	£4.30✓
B	Weston-super-Mare	£3.00
F	Pick your own	£2.00
	SATURDAY SEPTEMBER 15th	
+	Bournemouth	£5.30
	SUNDAY SEPTEMBER 16th	
A	Historic York	£5.00
B	Weston-super-Mare	£4.50
B	Exmouth	£5.50
D	Extended Cotswolds Tour	
	including light luncheon£	
	MONDAY SEPTEMBER 17th	
A	Blackpool "lights"	£5.00
B	Weston-super-Mare	£4.50
B	Clevedon	£4.50
	TUESDAY SEPTEMBER 18th	
B	Portsmouth & Southsea	£4.30✓
A	Skegness	£5.00
F	Malvern Hills	£4.50
	WEDNESDAY SEPTEMBER 19th	
B	London - 6 Hours stay	£5.00
B	Southampton and Solent	
	Cruise to Isle of Wight	£8.00
B	Weston-super-Mare	£4.50
	THURSDAY SEPTEMBER 20th	
A	Rhyl	£4.60
A	Historic Chester	£4.00
A	International Garden Festival	
	Liverpool. Inc admission	£7.50*
A	Southport Sands	£4.85
	FRIDAY SEPTEMBER 21st	
B	Bournemouth	£5.30
D	Stratford - market day	£2.00

	SATURDAY SEPTEMBER 22nd	
D	"Singing in the Rain" starring	
	Tommy Steel at the London	
	Palladium. Inc.seats	£12.75
+	Bournemouth	£5.30
	SUNDAY SEPTEMBER 23rd	
B	Weston-super-Mare	£4.50
B	Torquay	£5.50
C	Alton Towers including	
	admission and rides	£6.50
F	Half day in Evesham	£2.50
	MONDAY SEPTEMBER 24th	
B	Weston-super-Mare	£4.50
B	Cheddar Caves	£4.50
A	Rhyl	£4.60
A	Historic Chester	£4.00
F	Blackpool "lights"	£5.00
	RHINE VALLEY	
	5 Day tour by luxury Pullman	
	Coach. £130 inclusive. See	
	separate programme for details	
	TUESDAY SEPTEMBER 25th	
B	Barry Island	£4.75
B	Portsmouth & Southsea	£5.30
A	Barmouth	£4.75
D	Moreton-in-Marsh Market	£3.00

PRICES REDUCED FOR CHILDREN

* INTERNATIONAL GARDEN FESTIVAL
   LIVERPOOL
Senior Citizens & Child £5.50

	WEDNESDAY SEPTEMBER 26th	
B	Skegness	£5.00
B	Weston-super-Mare	£4.50
D	Slimbridge Wild Life	£3.00
D	Bristol Zoo	£3.50
F	Blackpool "lights"	£5.00
G	Over 50's Night Out with	
	supper and music	£3.50
	THURSDAY SEPTEMBER 27th	
A	International Garden Festival	
	Liverpool inc.admission	£7.50*
A	Southport Sands	£4.85
A	Rhyl	£4.60
A	Llandudno	£5.10
	FRIDAY SEPTEMBER 28th	
B	Weston-super-Mare	£4.50
B	Porthcawl & Coney Beach	£4.80
B	Bournemouth	£5.30
	SATURDAY SEPTEMBER 29th	
A	Blackpool "lights"	£5.00
+	Bournemouth	£5.30
	SUNDAY SEPTEMBER 30th	
A	International Garden Festival	
	Liverpool inc.admission	£7.50*
B	Weston-super-Mare	£4.50
A	Lake Windermere	£5.50
F	Afternoon Mystery Tour	£1.60
+	Evening Mystery Tour	£1.60

BARGAINS OF THE MONTH
ARE MARKED THUS ✓

4 WAYS TO ENJOY THE FUN OF BLACKPOOLS ILLUMINATIONS

NIGHTS OUT.......Every Wednesday and Saturday in October - Depart Birmingham 2.00pm - arrive Blackpool 5.00pm, tour of lights starts 10.30pm - arrive back in Birmingham approx' 2.30am

LONG DAY TRIPS...Every Saturday in October. Depart Birmingham 7.45am - Depart Blackpool 11.00pm.

THREE AND FIVE
   DAY TOURS ...Including accommodation and excursions.
             3 Days - £40, 5 Days - £68 inclusive.
             Please see separate programme for details.

September 1984 day trip programme.

The 1984 brochure cover featured a "Diamond" design to commemorate the company's 60th anniversary year.

Examples of inside pages from 1984 brochure.

1984 – A new coach for Jubilee year. WBV 529Y an ex demonstrator from Leyland – a Tiger 245 chassis with Jonckheere Jubilee P50 body. Large windscreen letters were now used for this and future vehicles.

Christened "Imperial Pullman" this coach had 49 reclining seats, toilet, double glazing, video and coffee machine.

WBV 529Y was later re-painted into Ivory fleet livery and received new registration UDL 222. It is seen here whilst on tour in Austria at the Stubai Glacier in 1986.

1986 – Another ex Leyland demonstrator purchased – B758 UHG - this time with the rear-engine Royal Tiger chassis and Van-Hool Alizee Super High body.

This coach had 49 reclining seats, toilet, double glazing, video and a coffee machine and was given the name "Imperial Diplomat".

B785 UHG seen whilst on tour in Ilfracombe.

After completing the 1988 tour to Turkey, B758 UHG was entered in the Showbus Rally at Woburn Abbey where it was awarded the Grey Green cup for "The best coach in show".

BIRMINGHAM TO TURKEY

Over the years Smiths coaches travelled the length and breath of the United Kingdom as well as making regular visits across the Channel to most parts of Northern Europe. During 1987 and 1988 two tours would take Smiths Leyland Royal Tiger – Van-Hool on the longest journey in the company's history.

These tours were undertaken during the summer months from Birmingham to Istanbul in Turkey travelling through France, Germany, Austria, Yugoslavia and making a stop en-route for 5 nights at Thessaloniki in Greece. After five nights in Istanbul the return route was via Bulgaria, Romania, Hungary – with 4 nights in Budapest and then home via Austria and Germany. A total of around 8,500 miles each tour was covered and the Leyland coach performed without fault.

Outward route: Birmingham – Calais – Frankfurt – Vienna – Zagreb – Belgrade – Thessaloniki – Istanbul.

Return route: Istanbul – Tarnovo – Brasov – Budapest – Salzburg – Karlsru – Calais – Birmingham.

Top - Approaching Budapest. Middle - Just 150km to our destination – Istanbul. Bottom - Bert Morton at the Greek and Turkish border.

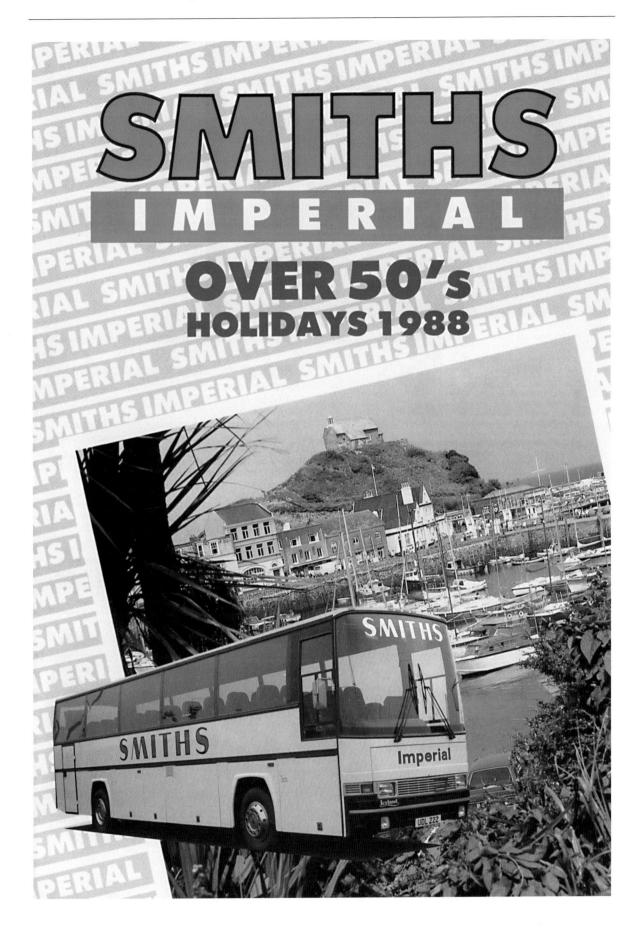

1988 Holiday brochure.

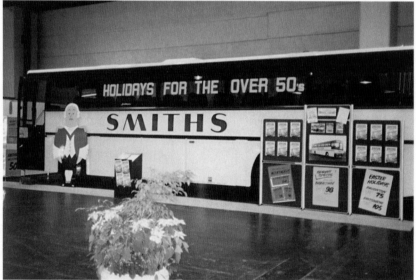

Drivers and staff present at the show...Peter Flannery, Andrew Roberts, Barry Smith, Bert Morton, Doreen Read, Robert Leight, Frank Knight and Roger Smith.

1989 – Holiday Show at the N.E.C., exhibition stand and UDL 222 was displayed to promote the 1989 holiday programme.

On tour - UDL 222 passing Goodreavy Lighthouse, Cornwall.

On tour - FJW 400V On the seafront at Boulogne.

1988 – F100 COM the last brand-new coach purchased, DAF SB2500 chassis with Duple 320SL body fitted with 57 reclining seats.

The only DAF coach purchased ran without fault until sold in 1997.

(top and bottom) 1990 – A752 GBA a Leyland Tiger 245 chassis with Plaxton "Paramount" 3200 53 seat body.

Unusually, for a Leyland Tiger, this vehicle was fitted with a "splitter" gearbox. It was previously operated by Woodward's Coaches of Glossop and later received YAU 400 registration.

B758 UHG was eventually re-painted into Ivory fleet livery and also received CIL 700 registration. Run by Smiths for 16 seasons this vehicle still had the original engine, including pistons & piston rings, when sold in December 2001 - must be a record for Leyland or were Smiths drivers just better than any others!!!

1997 – BAZ 6528 a Volvo B10M chassis with 53 seat Van-Hool Alizee body. Previously operated by Shearings this was the last coach to be purchased by Smiths.

Sample tickets and stationery – Clockwise from bottom left: Ticket wallet, Gift voucher, Luggage label, Day trip ticket, Letterhead.

2001 EDITION

SMITHS
IMPERIAL COACHES

COACH HOLIDAYS
Short Breaks and Weekends

We know how to look after you!

2001 – The last holiday brochure to be published.

"The final journey", Roger Smith is pictured with the famous Smiths logo just before closure of the business in December 2001.

The "flunkie" coachman, a familiar sight that stood on the forecourt for more than 40 years proclaimed, "Your coach is here madam". Now retired!

In the 1950's and 60's Smiths also offered remote-control garage door devices…just one of the many inventions that W.S.L. Smith dabbled with!